The Rebecca Riots
within
Ten Miles of Swansea

The Rebecca Riots within Ten Miles of Swansea

by

Derek Draisey

Draisey Publishing

DRAISEY PUBLISHING
73 Conway Road
Penlan
SWANSEA SA5 7AU

First published by Draisey Publications 2010
Copyright © Derek Draisey 2010

ISBN 978-0-9546544-6-7

Set in Minion Pro by Logaston Press HR3 6QH
and printed in Great Britain by
Bell & Bain Ltd., Glasgow

*Front cover illustration: Upper Sketty Cross toll-gate in the late
19th century. (Courtesy of West Glamorgan Archive Service)*

Contents

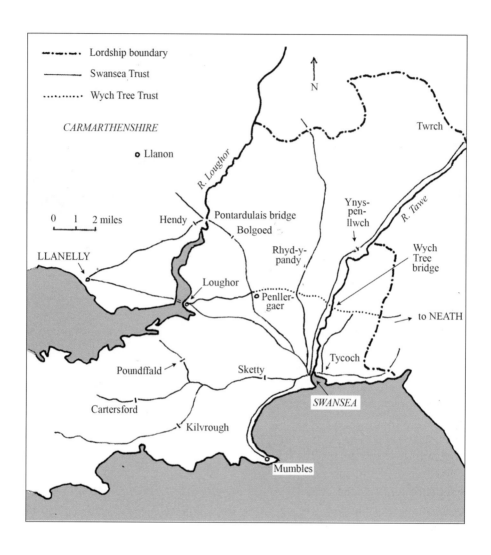

Map of the Lordship of Gower and Kilvey, showing the main turnpike roads of
the Swansea and the Wych Tree Bridge trusts. Also shown are
the positions of the toll-gates, bars and chains mentioned in the text,
although they are by no means all the barriers in the area.

Acknowledgments

Special thanks are due to the occupier of Cwmcillau-fach farm for allowing me to photograph the old farmhouse, and to residents in the vicinity for their willingness to engage in conversation about Rebecca's activities in the area. A special thank you is also due to staff at both the Penlan and Swansea Central libraries for their willing assistance, and also the Central Library itself because, without its *Cambrian* Index and microfilm, this work would never have been published. I am also grateful to Ron Shoesmith for preparing this work for publication at such short notice, and to Andy Johnson of Logaston Press for his willing assistance in matters pertaining to this publication.

Foreword

It has been estimated that the Rebecca Rioters were responsible for around 250 incidents, mainly attacks on toll-gates, toll-bars and toll-houses. The incidents dealt with in this work are those that took place in the Swansea area; that is, within the old Medieval Lordship of Gower and Kilvey, which extended northwards almost to Brynamman.

There are many varying accounts of what happened within the area specified above, but what is written here has been taken from reports that appeared in the locally-based newspaper, *The Cambrian*, between July 1843 and April 1844. The reports that appeared in this newspaper are not only enthralling, they are amazing for their attention to detail; they are also more reliable than other sources. In short, *The Cambrian* had a way of bringing what happened and the characters involved to life. Only a relatively small number of rioters were caught, but in respect to the Bolgoed and Rhyd-y-pandy gates the authorities were aided by an informer. His eye-witness accounts makes the newspaper reports all the more intriguing.

The attacks on the Poundffald gate, Three Crosses, and the Tycoch gate, St. Thomas, were also reported as eye-witness accounts, whereas that on the Pontardulais-bridge gate, which culminated in a 15-minute shootout between police and rioters, is brought to life by the testimonies of law enforcement officers involved in the bitter close-quarter fighting. Undoubtedly the most awe-inspiring reading of all is the desperate resistance to arrest that police officers encountered at Cwmcillau-fach farm, near Felindre. Eventually some 40 soldiers were deemed necessary to take the Morgan family into custody.

Memorable Dates
1843

6 July	attack on Bolgoed gate
15 July	attack on Poundffald gate
20 July	attack on Rhyd-y-pandy gate
22 July	informer contacts Inspector Rees
23 July	affray at Cwmcillau-fach farm
3 August	attack on Tycoch gate, St. Thomas
7 September	attack on Pontardulais gate
9 September	attack on Hendy gate
25 October	start of Commission of Inquiry
26 to 30 October	trials by Special Commission at Cardiff
7 December	the Pontardulais three leave Cardiff for Millbank Penitentiary, London

1844

6 March	publication of Report of Commission of Inquiry
mid-March	Glamorgan Spring Assizes

Rebecca

As to the name Rebecca – it was taken from Genesis 24, verse 60:

And they blessed Rebekah and said unto her, ...
let thy seed possess the gate of those
which hate them.

CHAPTER ONE

The Bigger Picture

In the 17th century and earlier, roads throughout Great Britain had been in a deplorable state until, in 1764, Parliament passed an Act to remedy the situation. The Act established the formation of trusts in which the well-to-do were permitted to invest money to improve and repair the main highways in their areas and to erect barriers for the collection of tolls. There can be no doubt that, in the first 75 years of their existence, the trusts greatly improved the condition of highways throughout the realm, but the tolls were resented by those who travelled frequently – particularly farmers.

Each trust set its own tolls and displayed the charges on a board attached to their toll-houses. The maximum that could be charged was fixed by the government and, from time to time, the maximum would be raised by subsequent Acts of Parliament. In 1839 a typical toll board might read:

For each horse drawing a carriage	6 pennies
For each horse not so employed	2 pennies
For each score of cattle	1 shilling 6 pennies
For each score of sheep	1 shilling

There were other charges, but what needs to be remembered is that one shilling is equivalent to five modern pence.

At first glance the charges do not appear exorbitant, but when one considers that, in 1839, the average wage of a farm labourer was ten shillings (50 modern pence) a week, it becomes apparent that paying the same tolls several times a day could be costly. No doubt everyone felt resentment when a toll-gate came into view on the road ahead, but moaning about it would not alter the situation; only direct action would. South Wales was already a hotbed of serious unrest in the 1830s and '40s. There was a series of bad harvests, food shortages, at least two trade depressions as well as frequent

1

strikes and riots in the industrialized areas. Moreover, workers had for a short time taken possession of Merthyr Tydfil, and extremists known as Scotch cattle were terrorizing Monmouthshire. Then there were the Chartists who were everywhere, demanding that the lower classes should have a say in government.

In the farming communities of West Wales there were grievances over paying high rents, church rates, tithes, poor law and tolls. The toll-gates were tangible objects against which farmers could vent their frustration. So it is hardly surprising that, in the summer of 1839, the grievances of paying tolls exploded into outright violence when farmers in West Wales began destroying the hated toll-gates and their attendant toll-houses. Their faces blackened and sometimes wearing women's clothes, the men involved in the unrest were referred to as Rebeccaites or Rebecca's Daughters, and their leaders were known as Rebecca or Becca.

The first spate of attacks was short-lived and no more was heard of Rebecca until October 1842. The second round of attacks began as somewhat humorous affairs with a degree of ritual, but in time the attacks became increasingly more frequent and more sinister. By the summer of 1843 Rebecca had turned her attention to other symbols of oppression, such as the hated workhouse at Carmarthen. The authorities offered rewards and free pardons to any activist who turned informer – to little or no avail. Then, in June, the military were called in and the situation went from bad to worse.

The Bolgoed Gate near Pontardulais

On Saturday the 8th of July 1842 the Swansea-based newspaper *The Cambrian* reported 'that the evil practices of toll-gate destruction, which have been so rife in Carmarthenshire, Cardiganshire and Pembrokeshire, have reached the borders of this county' (i.e. Glamorganshire).

> On the arrival of the mail-coach this morning from Carmarthen, the coachman informed us that ... the toll-bar and house at Bolgoed, near Pontardulais, were completely levelled with the ground. The furniture belonging to the house had been carried out, and placed on the side of the road.

The report was brief, but later evidence reveals that, on this occasion (Thursday the 6th of July), Rebecca was a local weaver, Daniel Lewis, who was probably employed at that time at one of several woollen mills in the Pontardulais area. Under Daniel Lewis's leadership, the attack on the Bolgoed gate (or toll-bar – the terms are interchangeable from *The Cambrian's* point of view) was a gentlemanly affair inasmuch as the toll-collector's furniture

The Fountain Inn, Bolgoed, near Pontardulais. On the main road near this historic inn stood the Bolgoed toll-gate. There is a story – though not in The Cambrian – *that the attack on this gate had been planned at several meetings held in this inn; also that the fiancée of Daniel Lewis, the local Rebecca leader, watched the attack from a window on the upper floor. A toll-bar is believed to have straddled the Goppa Road, which is to the left of the inn as you look at it. The purpose of the bar would have been to catch traffic from Goppa Fach. It has been said that a second attack was carried out on the (re-erected) Bolgoed gate, but there is no mention of this in* The Cambrian.

'had been carried out and placed on the side of the road' before the toll-house was demolished. The details of this attack, however, were provided by *The Cambrian* a month later – they were based on the evidence of an informer.

A Gentlemanly Attack

On Saturday the 5th of August *The Cambrian* reported on a preliminary investigation before magistrates 'at the Townhall, Swansea, on Wednesday 2nd August. The hall was completely filled' – everyone wanted to hear the evidence of one John Jones, an informer who had been present at the destruction of the Bolgoed toll-bar a month previously, on Thursday the 6th of July. The Chairman – who presided over the 18 magistrates present – asked the witness, John Jones, 'Can you speak English?'

'No, Sir,' Jones replied in English, which resulted in laughter. As Jones's English was deemed imperfect, a Mr. Glasbrook was sworn in as an interpreter. Jones stated: 'I live at Cwmsciach, in the parish of Llangyfelach ... I am a [farm] labourer'. At a later stage in the investigation he said, 'I [have] lived for the last six weeks in a barn belonging to Morgan Pugh'. Prior to that he lived at Pwllfa, but had been 'turned out of that house'.

The principal points of Jones's evidence were as follows:

> I saw the [Bolgoed] gate destroyed between twelve and one o'clock in the morning ... The parties engaged in the destruction ... amounted to some hundreds [later said to be 250] ... Some had white shirts on, and others had women's bed-gowns about them. They also wore women's caps ... There might have been a hundred guns there ... principally single-barrel guns, but some of them were double-barrelled ... They cut the toll-bar with cross-saws and hand-saws, and the toll-house they destroyed ... by ... taking out the lower stones with pickaxes [during which time] there was a continual firing of guns. They were occupied for about ten minutes in destroying both the toll-house and the toll-bar. Some of the parties had their faces disguised by having some kind of handkerchiefs tied around their heads, and hanging like veils over their faces. I did not observe that any of them had their faces blackened. One of the persons rode on a white horse. The men addressed the person on horseback by the name of 'mother.' I was near enough to the person they called 'mam' [mother] to hear them talk to him ... [he] had a white shirt put over his clothes. He had also a cap and bonnet on his head. He gave them directions, and made a short speech.

What John Jones did not say when he mentioned that Rebecca 'made a short speech' was that the speech was part of a ritual, which had its origin in *ceffyl pren* – a shaming ritual that was inflicted on anyone who was considered undesirable.

Referring to Rebecca, Jones pointed to a prisoner.

> That man [they called 'mam'] was the prisoner Daniel Lewis ... I know him to be a weaver and that he lives near the Goppa ... I saw more persons whom I knew among the mob. I saw Mr. Griffith Vaughan of the Pontardulais Inn ... He had a gun ... I saw David Jones of Dantwyn present ... I also saw John Morgan of Bolgoed ... I partly know where the crowd came. I first met them on the lowest part of Goppa mountain. This was between eleven and twelve o'clock ... They sat down on the mountain, and others came from all parts to join them ... I accompanied them to the gate ... Their numbers increased as they went on ... I had my coat turned inside out. I also put a handkerchief about my face. I did it for the purpose of being like the others ... They did not remain a minute

4

after they had destroyed the gate. They went together to the side of the Bolgoed mountain. They then pulled the bonnets, etc., from their heads and dispersed throughout the neighbourhood. I then went home.

Jones was cross-examined by several solicitors representing the four men whom he had informed on. There were a number of inconsistencies in his response compared with what he had said earlier, but what is important here is the evidence that sheds light on the events leading up to the destruction of the Bolgoed gate. Jones said that he had spent most of the day at his father's house, and from there he:

> went on an errand to my brother's. My brother's name is Richard Jones; he lives at Llanedi, in Carmarthenshire ... My brother was not in the house when I arrived, but came in there about an hour afterwards, accompanied by his wife ... When I left my brother's, I ... was on my way home [when] I heard that the Bolgoed bar was to be destroyed in that night ... I then went to Goppa Mountain ... I remained there for about half an hour. During that time the numbers increased ... One rose upon his feet and said to me, 'You know where we are going – it is to break down the Bolgoed gate'. It was Becca that said that. I knew who Becca then was ... I knew him by his voice [and] I had heard all the neighbourhood say that Daniel Lewis was to act Rebecca's character ... I turned the sleeves of my coat by the [woollen] factory, about three quarters of a mile from the Goppa mountain ... I was within three or four yards of the toll-house when it was demolished.

Apart from Daniel Lewis there were three other men whom Jones had informed on – 'David Jones, a farmer's son; William Morgan, a farmer [and] Griffith Vaughan of the Pontardulais Inn'. According to Mr. Maule, the Government Solicitor, all four men would be charged with a misdemeanour for their alleged involvement in 'the destruction of the Bolgoed gate'.

> [However] there was another circumstance which affected one of them – that was Vaughan ... a few days ago, a case [had] arrived by steam-packet from Bristol ... It was addressed to 'G Vaughan, Red Lion Inn, Pontardulais', and after he had been taken into custody ... the case was consequently detained and examined, and upon examination it was found to contain fire-arms and ammunition.

Speaking on Vaughan's behalf, a solicitor stated: 'Mr. Vaughan [has] denied having anything to do with the case in question. It was also irrelevant to the case', for the arrival of arms 'would be no' proof that Mr. Vaughan had 'destroyed' the gates.

In due course seven witnesses were called to prove that Jones 'was not worthy of credit'. These witnesses either rubbished parts of Jones's evidence, or said they 'would not believe him on his oath'. Jones's brother, Richard, said: 'I do not think my brother was in my house' on the day in question. At the end of the investigation, the four defendants were 'committed for trial at the next Assizes; and having entered into recognizance to appear at that time, were liberated'.

The Poundffald Gate, Three Crosses

The Cambrian reported Rebecca's next attack near Swansea on Saturday the 22nd of July. The newspaper stated that the attack was directed

> at the Poundffald gate near Three Crosses, Gower, on Friday night last, or rather early on Saturday morning [15th of July – nine days after the destruction of the Bolgoed gate], when a number of persons (some say about sixty, and others represent them as being many more) who had their faces blackened, and were otherwise disguised, amidst the firing of guns, entirely destroyed the gate, posts and all the 'appurtenances thereto pertaining,' excepting the toll-house, which they had ascertained belonged – not to the Trust ... but to Mr. Eaton, a farmer, residing near the place. The party also destroyed a chain, which was placed across a by-road, and intended as a kind of protection to the gate. A portion of wall along the road-side was pulled down. They sent the toll-collector to the house, and threatened to shoot him if he had the presumption to peep out either through the door or window. Mr. Eaton, the owner of the toll-house approached them, but he was soon compelled to retreat having been assailed by a volley of stones, pieces of gate, etc. It is reported that they had contemplated the destruction of another gate in the neighbourhood, but as dawn was approaching they abandoned their design.

The Cambrian also reported on the 22nd of July that:

> In consequence of the continued unsettled state of South Wales ... four 6-pounder field guns and two 12-pounder howitzers ... with ... men from the Royal Artillery ... were to proceed…to Carmarthen with the least possible delay ... On Monday, a company of the 75th Regiment of foot passed through [Bath] in four of the Great Western Railway carriages, as an additional reinforcement to the disturbed districts of Wales ... Two hundred of the 75th arrived in Swansea last night [Friday 21st] by the 'Bristol' steamer. How long they are to remain with us we have not heard. Billets have been taken for three days only ... As we were going to press, we learnt that the Rhydypandy gate and toll-house, two miles from Morriston, on the road to Clydach, were entirely destroyed.

The details relating to this attack were not published until two weeks later.

Upper Sketty Cross toll-gate in the late 19th century. This gate was one that survived for 30 years after the riots of 1842-43.

The Rhyd-y-pandy Gate

Mention has already been made of a preliminary examination before magistrates on Wednesday the 2nd of August, regarding the destruction of the Bolgoed gate. On the following day (Thursday the 3rd of August) another preliminary examination was carried out, one that gave details about the Rhyd-y-pandy toll-bar. Two brothers – Matthew and Henry Morgan – were 'charged with having formed part of the mob who had destroyed, on the 20th of July last, the above toll-bar'. It was the same John Jones who had informed on them. Jones deposed:

> Henry Morgan resides with his father at Cwmcillau-fach farm [on the hillside above Lliw Reservoir] and Matthew Morgan at Tymawr – three or four fields distant [to the east] from Cwmcillau ... [On] the night on which the Rhydypandy gate was broken ... I saw Henry first; that was at half past eleven ... I asked him if he was going to break the gate ... he replied that he was going to do like the rest ... Henry was dressed in a bedgown, and he had a kind of cap on his head, and a pickaxe in his hand. We went together across three or four fields, and arrived on the high road. I then stood on the road, and Henry went to the house of his brother Matthew. He came out of the house ... accompanied by Matthew. The latter was dressed in a bedgown, he also had a cap ... and ... a hatchet in

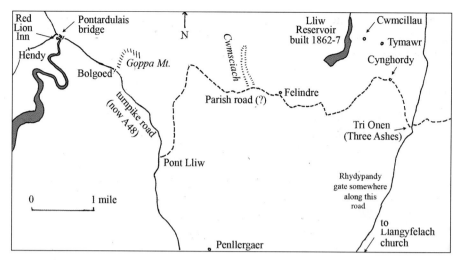

Map of the Pontardulais and Felindre area; it shows the toll-barriers, the farms and other places mentioned in the text.

his hand ... [we] went down the road [to] a place called Tri Onen [Three Ashes], where there are four cross-roads. We then went together to Coed-caebryn-maen; there were a number of people there – perhaps about forty.

There was one person there who attracted my attention ... they called him 'Becca' and 'mother' ... He rode a white horse, was dressed in a white shirt, and had something black over his face, and had a bonnet on his head. I did not recognize him ... The greater portion of the people had some instruments ... some had guns, some pickaxes, cross-saws, etc. They remained at Coed-caebryn-maen for about half an hour, and went off in a body towards Rhydypandy gate. The man on horseback went before them ... They arrived at the gate between twelve and one o'clock and then destroyed it – in ten minutes or a quarter of an hour ... I saw Matthew and Henry during that time. Henry Morgan drew off the board containing the terms of the gate, from the pine-end of the house. I heard them break it ... They then returned to Coed-caebryn-maen.

Jones lived in a barn at *Cwmsciach* (Cwm Ysgiach – a valley to the west of Felindre) with his 'wife and children', and it was reported that 'his wife declares that he was in bed on the night of the destruction of the Rhydypandy gate ... She also stated that, ever since the seizure of his effects for debt, his conduct has been such as to lead her to suspect that he is not altogether sane'. It appears that the reason for her last statement was that some of the Welsh 'have a notion, that if they can erect what they call "Ty un nos" – that is, if they can build a house on a common in one night unobserved – that the house so erected becomes their property. Jones erected a house of this description on a common ... over which Morgan of Cwmcillau had a right of pasturage, and which house' Morgan's sons, Matthew and Henry, had demolished.

It would, therefore, appear that Jones harboured a grudge against the brothers because, when cross-examined by a solicitor, he said:

> I never built a Tynos on a mountain. I dug the foundations of a house near Darren-fawr [near the Upper Lliw Reservoir]; that was last spring ... Mr. Jenkins of Cynhordy [Cynghordy, near Cwmcillau] afterwards went round the neighbourhood, and asked several persons to go with him to destroy what I had done. The two defendants went with them. I never said I would injure the defendants when I had the opportunity. I never said so either to John Williams of Penyfidy [near Felindre], or his wife.
>
> On the day of the destruction of the gate, I had been working at Gellywran issa [a farm about a mile from Cwmsciach] ... [I] left at nine o'clock.

What followed is confusing, but it would appear that Jones went home, then made for Cwmcillau, which is where Henry Morgan lived with his father. Jones said:

> I remained near Cwmcillau for a quarter of an hour, when I saw Henry Morgan ... I believe it was about eleven o'clock. I turned my coat in the field beyond Cwmcillau house.
>
> Mr. John Williams of Penfidy was examined and stated that, after the foundations on Darren-fawr had been destroyed, Jones said he would injure Morgan of Cwmcillau [father of the two brothers] or his children [Matthew and Henry] ... This conversation took place in May, in my own house.
>
> The defendants [Matthew and Henry] were then committed for trial at the next Assizes. – The Magistrates accepted bail to the same amount as that on which they had been previously liberated.

A contemporary illustration of an attack on a toll-gate.

CHAPTER TWO

Informed on

On Saturday the 22nd of July (two days after the destruction of the Rhyd-y-pandy gate) John Jones 'had business in Swansea. [He] intended having plates there', but went to Inspector Rees of the Borough Police to inform on the rioters. He had 'heard that a [£100] reward was offered for the apprehension of the Rebeccaites ... some days before'. Exactly what passed between him and Inspector Rees is not known, but he must have provided sufficient information for Rees to send for two magistrates. Jones maintained that the question of a reward did not arise until: 'I had asked Rees if I would be free if I informed on the others. Mr. Rees said I should have the reward if I could make out who had broken the gates'.

Right: *A Rural Policeman in 1843. His uniform was designed to create an image of authority – that is, of the 'boss' or a magistrate. It consisted of a stovepipe hat (which the well-to-do wore), a pilot-blue, swallow-tailed coat with the letter 'G' (for Glamorgan) and a number on the collar. The trousers were navy blue in winter, white in summer. He was issued with a new uniform each year, and was expected to wear it at all times, except in bed. The reason for this is that he was expected to devote himself to duty every day of the year. There was no such thing as leave, or rest days, until 1860 when he was awarded one week's annual leave and a few hours off for special reasons. His first pair of Wellington boots – which were issued – were a source of discomfort. In 1842 the issue was replaced by a weekly boot allowance of 6d.*

On Saturday night ... information was communicated to the Magistrates, relative to the parties implicated in the destruction of the toll-bars, in consequence of which, they issued warrants for the apprehension of several parties of the highest respectability ... Early on Sunday morning Captain Napier, accompanied by Inspector Rees of the Borough Police force, Sergeant Jenkins and Henry Lewis of the Rural Police, proceeded to the neighbourhood of Pontardulais with warrants for the apprehension of Mr. David Jones, son of Mr. Morgan Jones of Tymawr (formerly of Court-y-Carne), who is a most respectable freeholder, and Mr. William Morgan, farmer of Bolgoed. After having brought these two persons to town and placed them in custody ... the same officers proceeded to execute a warrant ... for the apprehension of Matthew and Henry Morgan, the sons of Mr. Morgan Morgan, a freeholder residing at Cwmcillau near Felindre ... The former resides on his own farm, which he rents from J. D. Llewelyn, Esq., and the latter, being a single man, in his father's house.

The Affray at Cwmcillau-fach Farm

The officers arrived at in the neighbourhood of Cwmcillau about nine o'clock in the morning, and apprehended Matthew Morgan at his own house, two or three fields distant from his father's house. He [Matthew] was left in the custody of Sergeant Jenkins and Lewis, while Captain Napier and Mr. [Inspector] Rees proceeded to Cwmcillau farm-house, for the purpose of executing the warrant against Henry Morgan. The nature of the warrant was fully explained in Welsh by Mr. Rees to the family, who positively declined allowing Henry to be taken by the officers. At last, Captain Napier and Mr. Rees found it necessary to take him [Henry] by force, when the whole family assisted in his rescue, and committed a serious assault upon Captain Napier.

The details of the assault are given below; suffice to say that the whole family ended up in custody.

On Monday morning [24th of July] Mr. Griffith Vaughan, formerly a draper in this town [Swansea], but now landlord of the Red Lion Inn, Pontardulais, and post master of that place, and Mr. Daniel Lewis [a weaver] known as a writer in the Welsh periodicals under the name of Petris Bach, were taken into custody on a charge of having been concerned in the destruction of the Bolgoed bar.

During the whole of Monday the town was in the greatest state of excitement, being filled with a number of respectable country people, farmers and others ... [Also] a private meeting of the Magistrates was held during the whole of Monday, in the Petty Sessions-room in the Townhall [now the site of the Dylan Thomas Centre, Somerset Place].

There were 17 magistrates present, among them Lewis Weston Dillwyn and his sons, J. D. Llewelyn of Penllergaer and L. Ll. Dillwyn, Thomas Penrice of Kilvrough and J. H. Vivian, M.P.. 'Several reporters made an application for admittance, but were told that the meeting was a strictly private one. Later it was announced that ... when the parties were brought up for a final hearing the public would be admitted'.

> On Tuesday morning [25th of July] the Magistrates commenced their public sitting soon after nine o'clock ... The following persons were then placed in the dock: Morgan Morgan and Esther Morgan, his wife, Rees Morgan and Margaret Morgan. There was also a charge against John Morgan, who was in the infirmary.
>
> Captain Napier, having been sworn in, made the following deposition: I am chief constable for this county. On Sunday last I proceeded to Cwmcillau ... for the purpose of executing a warrant ... for the apprehension of Matthew and Henry Morgan for the destruction of Rhydypandy gate ... I was accompanied by Inspector Rees of the Swansea Police, Sergeant Jenkins and [P.C.] H. Lewis of the Rural Police. We arrived at Cwmcillau at nine o'clock, and apprehended Matthew Morgan on the road near his own house, which is about three hundred yards distant from Cwmcillau. I left Matthew Morgan in the custody of Sergeant Jenkins and H. Lewis, and then proceeded, accompanied by Inspector Rees, across the fields to Cwmcillau farm-house. On arriving there, I directed Inspector Rees to ascertain if Henry Morgan was in the house. He went in the house.

At this point it is preferable to hear the later evidence of Inspector Rees; he deposed:

> Mrs. Morgan offered me a chair. I told them [the family, in Welsh] that I wished Henry to accompany me to his brother's house. The father said that his [Henry's] foot was bad, and that his brother must come to him. I told Morgan Morgan [the father] that Captain Napier was outside, and I asked Margaret [the daughter] to request him to come in, which she did.

Captain Napier deposed:

> I went with her into the house. The family offered me a chair ... When I sat down, Inspector Rees spoke to them in Welsh ... I then produced the warrant ... and desired Mr. Rees to explain to the parties the nature of it ... Inspector Rees informed me that the father stated that his son was lame and could not walk. I desired him to tell him that he [Henry] must come with us. Rees spoke to them in Welsh, and seemed to have some discussion with them.

13

At this juncture it is again preferable for Rees to take up the story. Rees deposed:

> I told Captain Napier, in English, what the old man had said – that he would lose his life before he would allow his son to be taken out of the house – and asked what was to be done. Captain Napier said, 'Lay hold of him'.

Captain Napier deposed:

> Rees proceeded to lay hold of Henry Morgan by the arm, and the whole family surrounded him and endeavoured to prevent his taking him from the corner in which he sat. Morgan Morgan, the father, and Esther, his wife, John Morgan ... Rees Morgan and Margaret Morgan, attacked him, and Henry finally succeeded in disengaging himself from Mr. Rees and attempted to run towards the stairs.
>
> I laid hold of him [Henry] by the collar, upon which the old man and his wife attacked me. The old woman [who was 63] jumped on my back, put her fingers in my eyes, scratched my face and bit my ear, while the old man took a stick and struck me repeatedly on the head ... The old woman then took an iron bar from the fire place and struck me several times on the head ... Margaret Morgan and [her brother John] attacked me. Margaret, after striking me on the head with a stick, took a saucepan, containing some boiling water, from the fire and poured it over my back. Eventually, I was compelled to let Henry Morgan go. They continued struggling with me until I got outside the door, when I fell.
>
> Previously to my falling I had taken a pistol from my pocket. When I was on the ground, the old man laid hold of my hand by the wrist and turned the muzzle of the pistol towards me, while John Morgan ... put his hand over mine and pressed the trigger with his finger. The pistol was not cocked ... the hammer being on the cap. The father had his right foot upon my thigh, and his left upon my groin, while John Morgan had his foot on the right side of my thigh, and was kicking me with the other foot, and by their endeavours they succeeded in turning the muzzle of the pistol towards my stomach, and kept pressing it to my body, while John Morgan continued pressing the trigger.
>
> At that moment I received a cut on my head with a reaping-hook from Margaret Morgan ... I had seen Margaret Morgan approach ... Considering my life was in danger, I turned the pistol, cocked it with my thumb and fired. I hit the young man, John Morgan ... He stepped backwards on receiving the ball, and again attacked me. I at last succeeded in getting to my feet, and observed Rees Morgan, who had a hammer in his possession, and Morgan Morgan, who had a reaping hook, approach me. I fired a second time into the air. No person received the shot.

One wonders what Inspector Rees was doing while Captain Napier fought for his life. Rees later deposed:

> I was pushed out [of the house] by Rees, Margaret and John Morgan. After I got out of the house, Rees Morgan took up this (producing a three pronged fish spear) with which he prevented my returning to the house. Margaret and John returned to the house and left Rees with me. In a short time I saw them bring out Captain Napier, who bled profusely from the head. They threw him against a wall, which was before the house. Margaret Morgan then brought the saucepan from the fire and threw some hot water at me, and then aimed several blows at my head with the edge of it; I warded them off with my club. Margaret Morgan went into the cart-house, from which she brought a reaping-hook (produced) and aimed a blow at the head of Captain Napier, while the father, mother and ... [John] kept him on the ground.
>
> At this time, I observed in Captain Napier's hand a pistol, the muzzle of which was turned towards his own body. Morgan and John Morgan struggled with him, as if to get the pistol out of his hand. I then heard a shot fired, upon which Captain Napier rose from the ground, and Henry Morgan came out with a hatchet (produced) ... Rees Morgan came after me with this hammer (produced – it was a large mason's hammer), which Captain Napier wrested from him, and with which he struck him [Rees Morgan] on the head. We then went to the field near the house, and Rees Morgan, Margaret Morgan and the old woman followed us. Rees had a pike, and Esther Morgan a stick, with which they aimed several blows, which I warded off. Sergeant Jenkins then came into the field and drew his sword [cutlass] with the flat part of which he struck Rees Morgan on the body.

Captain Napier's version of these later events was that, after he fired

> into the air ... Rees Morgan struck me with a hammer, and I knocked him down with my fist. Observing Henry Morgan running away, I directed Inspector Rees to follow him, which he did. I was following [Inspector] Rees, when Rees Morgan again interrupted me ... I again knocked him down with my fist. Inspector Rees then returned, having failed to apprehend Henry Morgan. Observing a mason's hammer in Rees Morgan's pocket, I attempted to get possession of it, but he retaliated and struck me with it. At length I succeeded in wrenching it from him, and struck him on the head with the hammer. He then left me alone. I afterwards directed Sergeant W. Jenkins and H. Lewis, who had arrived on the spot with Matthew Morgan, who had already been taken into custody, to bring John with them.

Captain Napier's final statement was:

> During the whole time Henry Morgan took no very active part in the assault, but appeared desirous of getting away.

Sergeant W. Jenkins stated:

> I heard a shot fired and went towards the house. Upon getting into the field before the house, I observed that Captain Napier was bleeding; his face and clothes were covered with blood. The four prisoners and Henry Morgan followed him. Margaret Morgan threw a stone. The old woman used a stick to me as soon as I approached them. Margaret tossed the hats of Captain Napier and Mr. [Inspector] Rees towards me, at the same time saying, 'Go home, you scamps and vagabonds.'

Cwmcillau-fach farm (2010). The dormer windows are of a much later age, but beneath the rendering is the original farmhouse where, as a family, the Morgans gave two police officers a hard time, preventing the arrest of a son and brother, Henry Morgan, who gave himself up two days later.
To the right is the yard – perhaps lowered, and now concreted over – where the two officers and the Morgan family spilled out of the house to continue struggling until a family member was shot. Forty soldiers turned up the following day to take the Morgan family into custody.

Captain Napier gave John Morgan, who was wounded, in charge to myself and Lewis. We handcuffed him to his brother Matthew and both were conveyed to Swansea.

Dr. Bird then testified as follows:

I examined Captain Napier's head at about eleven o'clock ... and found a cut on the left side, about two inches long, and down to the scalp-bone. There were also scratches on his face, and a mark on the right ear, which appeared to be that of a bite [later said to be 'on the left ear']. There were other bruises on the head. He also complained of a pain in the hip and walked lame.

The Cambrian provided the final information:

In the afternoon, three [horse-drawn] vehicles, with a party of the 73rd Regiment [40 soldiers according to L. Ll. Dillwyn] and several policemen, proceeded to Cwmcillau for the purpose of apprehending the rest of the family ... They succeeded in apprehending Esther Morgan, the mother, Margaret Morgan, the daughter, and Rees Morgan, one of the sons. Morgan Morgan was apprehended in

This farm building at Cwmcillau may have existed in 1843; the stonework provides a glimpse of what the original farmhouse may have looked like. The tithe apportionment of 1838 records that the father, Morgan Morgan, held 36 acres freehold in the immediate vicinity. He almost certainly held land elsewhere, possibly as a tenant of one of the big landowners such as John Dillwyn Llewelyn of Penllergaer. The tithe apportionment also records that the Cwmcillau property included a house and garden, as well as two cottages with gardens, which may have been used to accommodate farm labourers.

town, having come to enquire after his son [presumably John, who was wounded]. All the family were now in custody, with the exception of Henry Morgan [who had gone on the run and did not give himself up until Tuesday the 25th of July]. Dr. Bird and Mr. Rogers, surgeon, extracted the ball from John Morgan's body, and have done everything that was necessary for his recovery. The ball had entered the left side, below the navel, and was extracted from over the third lower rib, but the medical men were of the opinion that it had not entered the abdominal cavity.

Before the Magistrates

At the preliminary examination referred to above (Tuesday the 25th of July) an application was made for 'bailing the prisoners' (including those involved in the destruction of the Bolgoed gate). It was already established that 'breaking a turnpike-gate' was a misdemeanour. So the solicitor who made the application did so on the ground 'that there was nothing felonious in the rescue of Henry Morgan, consequently the prisoners would be committed [for trial in a higher court] for a misdemeanour, as the rescue of a prisoner could not be a higher crime than that with which the party (Henry Morgan) was charged'.

The Chairman of the magistrates, however, pointed out that certain 'parties had committed an aggravated assault' on Captain Napier; moreover 'the Magistrates were of the opinion that the parties could not be admitted to bail' until they had been committed for trial at a higher court. 'The prisoners were then remanded until the following morning. Henry Morgan ... surrendered in the course of the day by the advice of Mr. Walters [solicitor], and was in the dock during the latter part of the examination'.

On Wednesday morning (26th of July) 'the [Town] hall was as densely crowded as on the preceding day ...'

> The prisoners were placed at the bar, and the charge read over to them ... The Chairman ... announced that the Magistrates had come to a decision to liberate the parties [six men] who were in custody on a charge of destroying Rhydypandy and Bolgoed toll-bars, on their binding themselves respectively in the sum of £100, and two responsible sureties in £50 each, to appear on Wednesday next.
>
> Margaret Morgan, the daughter, was charged with having feloniously and maliciously assaulted Captain Napier, with the intention of preventing Henry Morgan from being lawfully apprehended. Morgan Morgan and Esther Morgan [the father and mother] and Rees Morgan, were charged with aiding and abetting Margaret Morgan, in the commission of a felony ... They were then committed to take their trial at the next Assizes.

All four members of the family bound themselves in the sum of £200 each, and each of them produced two sureties who bound themselves in the sum of £100 each, to appear at the next Assizes. 'The parties were then liberated'.

An application was made for the liberation of John Morgan, 'the young man [he was 21] who had been wounded, and who was then in the Infirmary of the House of Correction'. It was pointed out that bail was possible, but for the fact that John's case had not been heard. A lengthy conversation ensued. Finally it was agreed that several magistrates should proceed to the Infirmary to carry out an examination of John's case. As the charges against him were of a serious nature he was admitted bail on the same terms as his sister.

If the authorities at Swansea thought – apart from legal proceedings – that that was the end to the disturbances they were, within a week, to find themselves sadly mistaken. They were also to be surprised by the fact that the next attack took place right on their doorstep; moreover, it was not carried out by a farming community, but by colliers.

The Tycoch Gate, St. Thomas

On Saturday the 5th of August *The Cambrian* reported that:

> early on Thursday morning, it was generally rumoured in the town that the Tycoch gate, on the other side of the Swansea river, had been destroyed at about three o'clock on that morning, having been cut down with saws and other implements, and afterwards burnt on a lime kiln. The rumour, at first, excited considerable surprise, especially as ... it had occurred so soon after the long investigation before the Magistrates, on Wednesday, which terminated in the committal of the parties charged.
>
> In spite of the number of policemen, both rural and borough, at present adjourning in town – in spite of the number of the military, including companies of the 73rd and 75th Regiments, together with between forty and fifty Light Dragoons, the Tycoch gate ... was levelled to the ground unobserved, excepting by the toll-receiver who ... recognized one out of the thirty or forty rioters.

The Tycoch gate was said to have been 'in the parish of Llansamlet', but this may be an error. The location given was 'on the other side of the Swansea [Tawe] river ... about half a mile distant from Swansea [that is, the Borough of Swansea]' at a place where two roads met, 'one leading to Foxhole and the other to Danygraig', which places it in the hamlet of St. Thomas.

> One of the perpetrators ... had committed a most cowardly and disgraceful assault on Margaret Arnold, the toll-receiver ... a collier,

named David Lewis ... [has been] brought before the Magistrates. Reporters were admitted from the commencement of the examination, and the public generally shortly afterwards.

Margaret Arnold, having been sworn, stated that she was a single-woman, and collected tolls at Tycoch tollgate. When in bed about three o'clock this morning, I was disturbed by a noise outside ... Several heavy blows were given [to] the door ... and the shutters, the latter of which together with the windows had been smashed. When I ... opened the door, a man came from the turnpike towards me. He had an iron bar in his hand, with which he gave me a severe blow on the arm. I had held up my arm for the purpose of avoiding ... the blow on any other part. The prisoner, David Lewis, is the man who struck me ... and [I] ran into the house. He struck the door repeatedly ... until it was broken to pieces. I again went to the door, and observed the prisoner break down the toll-board which was fastened to the wall. There were about thirty or more men scattered ... about the house ... I screamed out 'murder' as loud as I could, upon which they all fled in various directions. They appeared to be working-men, colliers, etc., and were not disguised. One of the party rode a dark-coloured horse which appeared to be a cart-horse. In leaving he rode on before them ... I well knew the prisoner ... He had passed through the gate on the preceding afternoon with a cart. He rose his hand in passing, which intimated that he had no money ... but would pay again. I have frequently trusted him before, and he has always paid me.

A Mr. Melvin entered the room and 'said he appeared on behalf of the prisoner, and asked permission to cross-examine the ... witness'. Margaret's response to the cross-examination was that 'it was rather dark, but light enough for her to see his features ... She knew him well. He is rather lame'.

Mr. Melvin then offered to produce witnesses who could prove that the prisoner was in bed from nine o'clock on the ... night until five ... that morning'.

The magistrates did not wish to consider 'an alibi', but committed David Lewis 'for trial at the next Assizes on a charge of felony'; nor would they accept bail. David was committed to the House of Correction (the site now occupied by County Hall). A week later a Mr. Price made an application for bail on behalf of David, and did so on the ground that 'it was then August, and probably the assizes would not take place until the latter end of February, being seven months' imprisonment, which ... was a severe punishment even on the supposition that the man was guilty, but would be a very hard case, indeed, if he were innocent ... A brother and mother were dependent upon the prisoner and ... Mr. Price had certificates of good character from four of the prisoner's employers'.

'The Magistrates declined acceding to the application'. David spent almost eight months in 'the House of Correction'. What happened at his trial at the Glamorgan Spring Assizes is difficult to determine. One source maintains that he 'was discharged by proclamation', but an extensive search of *The Cambrian* has failed to confirm this statement.

Police Patrols

On Saturday the 19th of August *The Cambrian* reported that:

> as far as Glamorganshire is concerned the lady [Rebecca] has been pretty quiet during the last week ... The authorities are still on the alert, and we understand that several mounted and other police nightly watch the various toll-gates in the neighbourhood. One night last week the patrol which watched the Poundffald, and one or two other Gower gates, heard fifty or sixty gun shots fired by the Rebeccaites, who ... did not make their appearance, but the police declared that spies were sent by Rebecca's daughters to watch the movements of the patrols.

The same editorial also reported that, at a police committee held on Friday the 11th of August, 'a discussion [arose] respecting Jones, the informer, [and it was revealed that] since the information was given ... this individual had been living in the Inspector's room at the station-house ... [Several of those present] objected to keeping him in the station-house, [and did so on the ground that] if it were necessary to keep him in custody, either for protection or to ensure his attendance as a witness ... [then] he should be sent to the House of Correction'.

An artist's impression of an attack on a toll-gate from
the Illustrated London News *of the 11th of February 1843.*

CHAPTER THREE

With twelve people awaiting trial for their involvement in either the destruction of gates, or their assault on Captain Napier, the Welsh within the Lordship of Gower and Kilvey would appear to have lost their appetite for further unrest, as there was no serious trouble in the lordship for a period of five weeks. The West Walians, on the other hand, were by no means prepared to abandon the cause. It is, therefore, hardly surprising that later attacks on gates within the lordship were carried out by Rebaccaites from Carmarthenshire, by which time Rebecca's attacks were becoming increasingly more violent.

Shoot-out at Pontardulais

On Saturday the 9th of September *The Cambrian* reported an attack on the Pontardulais-bridge gate, which was situated on the Swansea side of the said bridge (today the site is marked by a plaque). The attack occurred during the night of Wednesday (the 6th) and the early hours of Thursday (the 7th of September). Almost all those involved would appear to have come from Carmarthenshire, where many were obliged to take part on account of threats by hard-liners. The newspaper obtained the following information from eye-witnesses.

> Rebecca notices were served calling upon the people to assemble on Wednesday near Llanon [in Carmarthenshire] ... At about half-past eleven o'clock ... the Rebeccaites assembled in a long body near Llanon ... As they marched along, they kept blowing their horns and firing their guns. An eye-witness says, there were at least one hundred horses ... most of them having two people on each – the procession being headed by Rebecca, and all her daughters being disguised in white dresses, bonnets and caps. Upon their arrival near Pontardulais they were heard by the gatekeeper ... and about one o'clock ... [in the] morning he was alarmed by shouts and the firing

of guns. They were about a mile off when he first heard them. He immediately removed the rest of his furniture into the garden at the back of his house, which he saved. When he saw the mob ... coming towards him, he ... ran to hide himself in a field about one hundred yards from the gate. Arriving at the gate, they immediately proceeded to pull it down: one gate was broken to pieces ... The windows and door of the house were smashed in, and the inside completely gutted; a part of the wall of the house was also pulled down, showing that a few minutes longer would have sufficed to raze it to the ground.

Pontardulais Bridge (2010). This is a modern replacement of the bridge that stood here in 1843. On the far side (on the left) is the Red Lion Inn, which is several times mentioned in the text. The toll-gate stood approximately on the spot where this photograph was taken (on the Swansea side of the original bridge).

The authorities were aware of Rebecca's intentions. Their response was twofold – to send magistrates, police and troops from Swansea to Pontardulais, and to dispatch magistrates and troops from Llanelly to the Hendy-bridge gate on the Carmarthen side of the River Loughor. The purpose of the magistrates' involvement was to provide civil guidance on which the troops could act. With regard to the forces of law and order from Swansea *The Cambrian* provides the following account.

Information was received by the authorities on Wednesday [6th of September] that an attack upon the Pontardulais gate had been contemplated, and was to be carried into effect during the night. A force of Rural Police, consisting of Mr. Superintendent Peake, two sergeants, and four policemen proceeded towards that place. They were soon afterwards joined by Captain Napier, J. D. Llewelyn (of Penllergaer), L. Ll. Dillwyn, Esqs., and accompanied by Matthew Moggridge, Esq. and Mr. Attwood. When about two or three fields distant from Pontardulais, they heard the firing of guns, rockets, the blowing horns and the noise of a great number of horses, more resembling a cavalry regiment than a party of Rebeccaites. It is stated that with the blowing of ox-horns, tin-horns and different other wind instruments, in addition to the feigned voices – resembling a host of old market-women, they made a most hideous and indescribable noise.

The party came from the direction of Llanon [in Carmarthenshire]. After having given three cheers when opposite the Pontardulais [Red Lion] Inn, they arrived at the gate, which was but a short distance from the inn. They commenced an attack upon it with saws, sledges, etc., and soon succeeded in breaking down the gate, as well as the side-rails, and also commenced demolishing the house, having broken the windows and a portion of the corner of the houses nearest the inn, they had also knocked in the door, but the [gate] posts had not been cut down.

When the work of destruction had proceeded thus far, the Magistrates and the Police, who were well armed, advanced. The Rebeccaites assembled at this time was estimated to consist of 150 to 200 persons, the majority of whom were on horseback. They were all disguised, many of them having their faces blackened and dressed in women's clothes; others wore bonnets, white shirts, and some appeared to have their coats turned [and some had their faces concealed with ferns]. Becca, on this occasion, was mounted and wore a large white cloak. When the Police appeared, the rioters immediately fired a volley at them, but fortunately without effect. The Police immediately fired in return. The distance between the constables and the rioters did not now exceed ten to fifteen yards. A desperate conflict ensued, which lasted about fifteen minutes, when the mob commenced retreating and flying in all directions. The groans of several of the wounded were distinctly heard.

The mob having dispersed, it was found that three of them had been captured, together with their horses, and among them the renowned Rebecca, who was found dangerously wounded on the bridge ... His name is John Hughes, the son of a farmer residing in the neighbourhood of Llanon [near Tumble]. Another person, named David Jones, was also dangerously wounded. In the course of quarter of an hour the Dragoons, who had been dispatched from Swansea, arrived. Four of the rioters who attempted to make their escape were also apprehended, having been met by a party of infantry, who were coming from Llanelly. The four were secured and brought back to Pontardulais, but were subsequently taken to Llanelly.

It has been stated ... that the rioters had placed sentinels on horseback, in several parts of the road, at a distance of two miles from the gate, expecting that the Dragoons would be their pursuers, but their tactics were entirely baffled, as Magistrates and Police proceeded across the fields, which could not have been well done by horsemen.

The wounded men were immediately attended to by Dr. Bird, who ordered them to be conveyed on stretchers to the Infirmary of the Swansea House of Correction. Both of them are in a very precarious – some say, dying state. It appeared that John Hughes had received a gunshot on the left arm, on the outside of the elbow joint. The ball, which was quite flattened when extracted, had passed upwards from the elbow, shattering the bone on the arm at its lower end, and was extracted at the back part of the same arm, midway between the shoulder and the elbow; he had also a contused wound on the head. There is a doubt as to the possibility of eventually saving the wounded arm ... David Jones, the other wounded man ... had received several wounds in the back, which appear to have been inflicted by shot, or slugs, a circumstance which proves that ... the rioters fired at each other, for the police used neither slugs nor shot. Jones has also been stabbed, and had three wounds on the head, which had been apparently inflicted with swords.

In the pocket of the leader was found a threatening note: Daniel Jones of Brynhir – meet me at Llan on Wednesday night; if you don't, this shall be your last notice. – Becca.

At a later date *The Cambrian* reported on an investigation in which Captain Napier gave evidence. The evidence provides detailed information about what happened at Pontardulais, as seen through the eyes of Captain Napier. The evidence also makes it plain that Napier – who had recovered from the injuries he received at Cwmcillau-fach farm – was once again prepared to put himself and those with him at risk. At the investigation he deposed:

> In consequence of information received, I went, accompanied by Mr. Super-intendent Peake, two sergeants and four police-constables, to Pontardulais ... on Wednesday last [he was also accompanied by four civilians]. We arrived at Pontardulais a little before one o'clock on the following morning. Just before we entered the village, I heard ... horns blowing and great many guns fired off. I also heard a voice, like that of a woman, crying out – 'Come, come, come', and a voice like the mewing of cats. This noise appeared to ... proceed from the direction of the Red Lion Inn, which is a short distance from the turnpike-gate. Immediately after this I heard a voice crying out loud – 'Gate' and in a very short time afterwards I heard a noise, as if the gate was being destroyed.

A memorial to the Rebecca Riots of 1843. It stands in Pontardulais, near the bridge over the River Loughor. It is one of several memorials that have been erected in the area.

I then proceeded with my officers and men towards the gate, and on coming into full view, I observed a number of men mounted ... and disguised ... Most of them appeared to be dressed like women, with their faces blackened. A portion of the men were dismounted and in the act of breaking the gate and the toll-house. About three of them, who [were on the Swansea side of the gate] appeared to lead, were mounted, having their horses' head towards the gate, and their backs towards me. At this time there was a continual firing of guns kept up by the parties assembled [on the far side of the gates]. I immediately called on my men to fall in and proceed towards the [three] men who were on horseback ... and called upon them, as loud as I could, to 'Stop'.

Upon coming up to them, one of the mounted men ... turned round and fired a pistol at me. I was close to him at the time. I moved on a few paces, and a volley was fired by the parties assembled in the direction of the police. I should say the volley was fired at us ... The three men on horseback [then] rode at us, as if they intended to ride us down ... I fired at, and shot the horse on which [rode] the man ... who had fired his pistol at me. A general skirmish ensued, during which a number of shots were fired on both sides I then endeavoured to take the parties, the three mounted men in particular, into custody ... The three prisoners, John Hughes, David Jones and John Hugh were ... taken into custody, after a very considerable resistance on the part of David Jones and John Hughes ... [and] in a short space of time the rioters were dispersed.

When cross-examined, Captain Napier maintained that 'the prisoner, John Hughes, is the person who fired the pistol at me ... To the best of my belief the prisoner, John Hughes, is one of the three persons who rode at us ... As to David Jones – I saw him very violently resisting Mr. Lewis Llewelyn Dillwyn, the Magistrate, and the police officers. He was struck several times upon the head before he was taken'.

The police officers who were present also testified at the investigation. Some of their evidence is contradictory in that more than one constable claimed to have captured the same prisoner. P. C. Wright, for example, deposed that 'the prisoner, John Hughes ... had a gun in his hand. I saw him fire towards the police ... I kept my eye on him. He fell, or got off his horse, and ran away with the horse [whereas Captain Napier maintained that he shot the horse]. His gun fell, which I immediately picked up'.

P. C. Price, on the other hand, deposed:

I took a man from his horse. That man was the prisoner, John Hughes. I gave him in charge to Sergeant Jenkins. I then took the prisoner, John Hugh, who has a broken arm [which was incorrect]. He was on horseback in front of the mob ... He had a gun ... The gun was pointed towards us when he discharged it. I was ten to fifteen yards from him when he fired ... I took him into custody near the Pontardulais Inn.

John Hughes and John Hugh were two of the horsemen who rode at the police. What happened to the third horseman is unknown. He may have been the one who came into conflict with P. C. Jones, who deposed: 'I ran into the crowd and took a gun from one man, who was on horseback. The man made his escape ... he galloped off'.

David Jones, the third man to be taken prisoner, was not one of the three horsemen. As the report in *The Cambrian* recounted, he is known to have been wounded several times in the back through being hit by gunshot, or slugs, which the paper noted proved that the rioters had fired at each other, as the police used neither shot nor slugs. Jones had also been stabbed, and had what appeared to be three sword wounds to the head. In his evidence, Captain Napier said: 'I had seen the prisoner, David Jones, with a stout stick in his hand, with which he aimed a blow at Lewis Llewelyn Dillwyn, Esq., a Magistrate'. Napier's evidence does not, however, account for the multiple injuries that Jones received; nor does the evidence of two constables.

P. C. Williams testified: 'I saw David Jones and another man coming out of the toll-house. The former struck me with an iron bar ... I then cut him on the head with my cutlass ... he ran away and Sergeant George Jones apprehended him'.

This was not quite how Sergeant George Jones remembered the incident; he stated: 'the first thing which particularly attracted my attention was David Jones running out of the toll-house. I pursued him and laid hold of him. A scuffle ensued, and he got from me. I again laid hold of him, and succeeded in keeping him in custody, and handcuffed him'.

The Cambrian reported that the affray had 'lasted about fifteen minutes, when the mob commenced retreating and flying in all directions. The groans of several of the wounded were distinctly heard ... In the course of quarter of an hour the Dragoons, who had been dispatched from Swansea, arrived'. These Dragoons were late (one source says they arrived up to one hour after the affray), but were sent in pursuit of the mob. They caught no one, but after they had crossed the bridge over the River Loughor they made contact with the forces of law and order from Llanelly.

The Llanelly Contingent

While Captain Napier engaged with rioters at Pontardulais, there were other events taking place on the Carmarthen side of the River Loughor. What happened there is to be found in the evidence of Mr. W. Chambers, Esq., who deposed:

I am one of the Justices of the Peace for the county of Carmarthen. In consequence of information received, I proceeded from Llanelly, accompanied by Capt. Scott of the 76th Regiment and a body of [between 20 and 30] soldiers, towards the neighbourhood of Pontardulais. We set out from Llanelly, which is six or seven miles distant ... at about ten o'clock.

Before arriving at Gwilly bridge, which is three quarters of a mile distant from Pontardulais, I heard ... the firing of arms ... in the direction of Pontardulais bridge ... I requested Capt. Scott to load. I then advanced ... and saw the prisoner, Lewis Davies, coming ... towards where I was. I immediately collared him ... his face was ... blackened ... I then gave him into the charge of Sergeant Gibbs ... I then went with the rest of the men ... [towards] Hendy-bridge gate ... which I had gone to protect.

Finding them [the rioters] not arriving, I was surprised. I also heard the galloping of horse on the Swansea road ... About the same time I heard the trampling of feet ... One of the persons walking got to the gate [where we were] and perceiving the soldiers, he ran back. They [the soldiers] pursued him and overtook him ... He was a boy, Wm. Hugh ... He was dressed in women's clothes ... and his face was blackened. I then went towards Pontardulais, accompanied by Capt. Scott and the soldiers. On arriving at the bridge, the Dragoons from Swansea were coming up – we thought they would have charged us, mistaking us for Rebeccaites. We found the turnpike-gate ... at that place destroyed.

Sergeant Gibbs deposed:

on standing with three other soldiers [and the prisoner Lewis Davies], I saw two men, whom I stopped ... Thomas Williams and Henry Rogers. I apprehended them ... They were neither disguised nor armed ... they said that they had nothing to do with the gate, but only went to look on.

Before the Magistrates

On Saturday the 9th of September, at the House of Correction, Swansea, nine magistrates carried out a private investigation 'into the charges against John Hughes, John Hugh and David Jones', for their involvement in the destruction of the Pontardulais gate. The depositions (written statements) of some witnesses at this investigation have been briefly touched upon.

On the following Monday the above prisoners were present 'at the Townhall for public examination. John Hughes appeared with his arm in a sling, David Jones with his head bound up, and John Hugh in his gown and straw hat'. John Hughes, alias Jac Ty Isha, was the son of a 'very respectable farmer', whose farm (Ty Isha) was situated near Tumble in Carmarthenshire. John was about 24 years old, fairly well educated and described as hale, powerful and good looking. There can be little doubt that, at Pontardulais, he was Rebecca. John Hugh was 'the son of a farmer residing' near Llanon. He was a year older than John Hughes, is said to have been married and could read a little. Of David Jones little is known, other than that he was about 21 and probably illiterate.

As to the four men taken by the Llanelly contingent, Lewis Davis (the first to be apprehended) claimed 'that he was compelled to accompany the mob by threats from ten or twelve persons, who called for him with guns ...' The 14-year-old boy, William Hugh, the son of a farmer, maintained 'that while he was in bed, a crowd of persons came to his house ... and compelled him to go with them. He proceeded to put on his own clothes, and they dressed him in women's clothes, and put in his hand the horn which was found on him. When an opportunity offered, he turned back and ... met the soldiers who apprehended him'.

'The prisoner, Henry Rogers, said he was a farm servant ... and only went to see the mob. Thomas Williams, servant to John Thomas, Llangennech Mill, said that he accompanied Rogers to see them, and was apprehended in returning home'. Neither of these two men were disguised; nor were they wearing women's clothes when they were taken into custody. 'The Chairman [chief magistrate] informed Rogers and Williams that they would be discharged ... as the evidence was not sufficiently clear to warrant their committal; still the magistrates were convinced that they were out for no good purpose at that hour of the night. After some further suitable admonition, both were discharged. Lewis Davies and the boy Hugh were remanded until Tuesday' [the 12th of September]. On that day:

> the prisoners John Hughes, David Jones and John Hugh, were brought up at the Townhall for [a] final examination. The Clerk of the Magistrates read the charges against them, which was to the effect – that they, together with divers other evil-disposed persons ... did unlawfully, riotously and tumultuously assemble together, and did then and there feloniously and unlawfully, and by force, begin to demolish and pull down the house of William Lewis [the toll-collector].
>
> There was another charge against John Hughes, charging him with having ... a certain pistol loaded with gunpowder and shot, which he held in his right hand at and against one Charles Frederick Napier, feloniously and unlawfully did shoot, with the intention feloniously, wilfully and of malice afterthought, the said Charles Frederick Napier to kill and murder, and David Jones and John Hugh with having ... been feloniously present, aiding, abetting and assisting the said John Hughes in the felony aforesaid to commit.

31

The Chairman then informed the prisoners that they stood committed for trial at the next Assizes to be holden for this county, the first three prisoners for felony, the two latter [Lewis Davies and the boy Hugh] for misdemeanour.

The latter two prisoners were admitted to bail. There were now a total of 17 persons awaiting trial for offences committed within the Lordship of Gower and Kilvey.

The Hendy Gate

Although in Carmarthenshire, the Hendy gate was only a half-mile or so to the east of the River Loughor, which served as the boundary between the County of Carmarthen and the Lordship of Gower. The gate's close proximity to Pontardulais, coupled with the fact that, in the minds of local people, it is linked with riots in the Pontardulais area, demands that it should be included in this work. The attack on the Hendy gate took place only two nights after the one on the Pontardulais-bridge gate and it, therefore, seems likely that Rebecca and her Daughters had intended destroying both gates on the same night, only to be thwarted by Captain Napier; hence Rebecca's return two nights later.

Between eleven and twelve o'clock on the evening of Saturday 9th September, the gate and toll-house at Hendy were destroyed. According to *The Cambrian*, 'the number of persons [Rebeccaites] assembled could not have been great, as ... neither the noise of horses nor the trampling of feet was heard ... [only] five or six gunshots'. The toll-house 'had a thatched roof and contained two rooms'. So it is probable that the perpetrators simply torched the roof, with the result that the toll-collector, 75-year-old Sarah Williams, went to a neighbour's house 'to seek assistance, after which she returned to the toll-house' to remove her furniture; that was the occasion in which she was shot.

At an inquest held on Tuesday the 12th of September the first witness was John Thomas, 'a house carpenter, residing near the Hendy gate toll-house'. Thomas deposed:

> Late on Saturday night last ... I was alarmed by ... the report of five or six guns near the Hendy gate. I was then in bed, and soon afterwards Sarah Williams, the deceased, came to my house to call me and my family to assist her to put out the fire ... but we did not go ... as we were afraid to do so ... [Later] I heard the report of another gun, and in about a minute afterwards the deceased came to my house [again] and my wife went to the door and saw the deceased coming towards her ... crawling along by the wall, against which she leaned to support herself, until she came to the door, when she cried out, 'dear, dear', and fell down. I then found she was dead.

Margaret Thomas, wife of the last witness, said,

> that ... between eleven and twelve o'clock last Saturday night, the
> deceased came to our house and asked my husband and myself
> to get up directly, as some persons had set her toll-house on fire.
> I went out to the door and told her to carry her things out of the
> house. She went back to the toll-house, and took part of her furni-
> ture and placed it on the road. I repeatedly asked her to come to
> our house, but she did not come. I heard the report of four or five
> guns soon afterwards, and the deceased, in about three quarters of
> an hour ... came towards my house, at which time I was standing
> at the door ... The deceased did not speak a word that I heard; and
> seeing that she was exhausted, I laid hold of her round the waist.
> She sank down at my door, on the outside. My husband then came
> out, and we took her into the house, but she did not speak a word.
> My husband held her, and put her to sit upon the floor, and she
> died in about two minutes after. I saw no blood, with the exception
> of a little on her forehead ... I did not think from the blood I saw
> on her forehead, that she might have had a blow which killed her. I
> thought ... that she did not die from a blow ... but from suffocation,
> occasioned by loss of breath.

Mr. Benjamin Thomas, [after being] sworn and examined [said]:

> I am a surgeon residing at Llanelly. I have, in company with Mr.
> Cook, made a 'post-mortem' examination of the body of Sarah
> Williams, the deceased, now lying at the Black Horse, Pontardulais.
> We examined the body, both externally and internally ... The marks
> of shots were seen penetrating the nipple of her left breast – one in
> the armpit of the same side – several shot marks in both arms – one
> on the left side of her windpipe – several on the forehead – and one
> in the external angle of the right eye. There was blood on her clothes
> ... In moving the body to a sitting posture a considerable quantity of
> blood escaped from the mouth.

From here on the surgeon's testimony is particularly gory; suffice to say that
he found 'about three pints of blood' in the lungs.

'The Jury then retired to consider their verdict and, after almost a
quarter of an hour, brought in the following verdict: "That the deceased died
from the effusion of blood into the chest, which occasioned suffocation – but
from what cause is to this Jury unknown" '. The verdict was not approved of
by the authorities; it showed that the local Welsh could not be trusted to be
impartial jurors in any forthcoming trials.

Shoni 'Sgubor Fawr

There had been a great deal of anger over the shootout at Pontardulais because, it was said, 'several farmers ... are dangerously ill of wounds received ... in that encounter ... [but] very few – if any – expressed regret for [Sarah Williams's] death'. Her killer, however, was not entirely unknown.

Throughout August and September a criminal gang had been operating in the Gwendraeth Valley (between Llanelly and Carmarthen). The gang had been led by a drunken bully known as *Shoni 'Sgubor Fawr*. Shoni not only carried out attacks in the name of Rebecca, but he practised 'a kind of blackmail' upon farmers whom he knew to be Rebeccaites. After his arrest on the 28th of September, Shoni informed on his associates.

It is believed that only a dozen men were involved in torching the toll-house at Hendy – more or less the number of men in Shoni's gang. There were no horns blowing, no ritual in this attack, just five or six gunshots. Shoni was not present and, therefore, not an eye-witness to the event, but he had heard that Sarah Williams had been accidentally shot by John the Shoemaker of Horeb, a member of his gang.

CHAPTER FOUR

The Turnpike Trusts

There were two turnpike trusts within the Lordship of Gower and Kilvey – the Swansea Turnpike Trust and the Wych Tree Bridge Trust, the former being by far the larger of the two, responsible for 77 miles of turnpike roads, including three miles in Swansea. On Thursday the 7th of September the Swansea Trust – which consisted of '65 Trustees, all of whom were either magistrates, land-lords or landowners' – held a meeting with a view 'to afford all possible relief to toll-payers'.

The main resolution involved taking over the smaller Wych Tree Bridge Trust – which was responsible for the bridge and 2½ miles of road on either side of it – with a view to discontinuing the gate there on the 1st of October. It was also proposed to discontinue the Poundffald, Bolgoed and Rhyd-y-pandy gates, and also the 'bar at Penfilia, which was merely a chain for the purpose of catching persons with coal'.

Ynyspenllwch Gate		
Clears Twrch Gate		
		168
	s.	d.
Waggon		
Cart...		
Coach, chaise, &c		
Gig		
Horses		
Cattle		
Sheep, Pigs		
Asses..		

Toll-gate tickets such as this may have been used by the Swansea Turnpike Trust.

The gates that were to remain in use were: Cartersford (on the North Gower Road), Kilvrough (where the trust had taken 'it upon themselves the repairs of four or five miles of road from Park[mill] to Reynoldston'), Loughor ('as material improvements had been effected upon that road') and Pontardulais-bridge ('which was a very good one'); also 'that a ticket from the Ynyspenllwch gate [Clydach] should clear the Twrch [gate in the Upper Swansea Valley] and vise versa'.

The gates mentioned above were by no means the only ones within the Lordship of Gower and Kilvey. There were, for example, gates at St. Thomas, the Hafod, Sketty and many more elsewhere. It should also be pointed out that some of – if not all – the gates mentioned at the above meeting were not managed by the trustees, but were contracted out to one Thomas Bullen, and he would need to be reimbursed for his loss of income.

The proposals referred to above were debated. One trustee opposed the proposals on the ground that, although he knew that certain gates would be discontinued 'because no great profit was received from them ... the farmers would always retain in their minds the notion that the Trustees were actuated by fear'. Another trustee declared that he would have been of the same opinion, but for the fact 'that Rebecca had [suffered] a serious check on the preceding night [at Pontardulais, and now thought] it time to make concessions'. Finally, a vote was taken and the proposals were adopted.

The Turnpike Highway

Once a highway had been levelled and the potholes filled in, the surface was covered in a thick layer of limestone rubble. The resulting road might be 24 feet (8 metres) wide to allow cattle and carriages to pass in opposite directions. The road might be flanked by drainage ditches, and beyond that there would often be walls, hedges or banks to prevent evasion of tolls. In time the limestone rubble would be ground to dust, and the road had to be resurfaced. In summer the dust could be a real source of annoyance to anyone residing near the road. Tarmac did not begin to replace limestone until the first decade of the 20th century.

Rebecca's New Tactics

The shootout at Pontardulais would appear to have instilled caution among local Rebeccaites, but it did not deter them from pursuing their cause in a different way. On Saturday the 23rd of September *The Cambrian* reported:

> in our last [issue] ... the [rebuilt] Pontardulais gate ... had been carried away a few days after [the shootout] ... Since then the Trustees caused a bar to be erected there as a temporary substitute for a gate. In consequence of an intimation received by the authorities of an

intended attack upon the bar on Saturday night, it was sedulously watched on that night, and as a matter of course, Rebecca was not seen; but, on the following night (Sunday), when the military had quitted their posts, Rebecca removed the bar. Since which, a chain ... placed across the road has also been carried away, and on Tuesday night last, another bar was removed. On Wednesday, a pair of new gates were erected there, but how long they shall stand remains to be seen. We fear they must share the fate of their predecessors.

Since the first destruction of the gate, no tolls have been collected during the night, the collector deeming it the best part of valour to retire soon after sunset, and attend early on the following morning. However, it appears that he was not at his post early on Saturday morning, as a number of farmers and others who attended Swansea Market, meeting with no obstruction in the shape of a toll-gate or even a toll-collector, passed toll free. In the afternoon, as the farmers were returning, the collector demanded payment from those who had paid no toll in the early part of the day ... Some persons paid, but others insisted upon passing toll free. Since then, the collector has received a threatening letter from Becca, advising him to quit, or he must take the consequences of incurring her displeasure.

The Military

In a letter to the P.M., dated the 26th of September, the Home Secretary criticized Colonel Love, C-in-C of all forces in South Wales, for his handling of the situation. The letter stated:

> Colonel Love has under his command a Force of 1,800 men ... I am not satisfied with the use he makes of this Force. It is quite sufficient to conquer the four counties, which he is asked only to keep quiet in aid of the Civil Power, but it so happens that he keeps the troops constantly in motion and always arrives too late. If a crime be committed, he instantly sends soldiers to the place on the 'following' day. The troops are thus constantly paraded before the People with apparent impotence and the authorities are brought into contempt.

Contingents of dragoon and red-coated infantry were garrisoned at Swansea. Some of them may have been billeted in the defunct townhall in front of the castle, and even in the castle itself. Many of them were almost certainly billeted in alehouses and inns, but whatever premises were used must have been considered inadequate, for on Saturday the 23rd of September *The Cambrian* reported that, on the previous Monday,

> a meeting of Magistrates was held at Mr. Attwood's office, to take into consideration the course to be pursued with respect to the providing of barracks for the troops now stationed at Swansea. It will

be remembered that, Col. Love having intimated his determination of withdrawing the troops from the town, unless proper accommodation were provided for them, the Magistrates applied to the Town Council for funds with which to erect temporary barracks; but ... the Council ... decided that no additional ... troops were required ... in consequence of this refusal ... the Magistrates have determined upon converting into barracks the house in High Street known as the 'London Hotel', and which is used at present as a night asylum for the homeless poor. As it was stated ... that the Magistrates had no available funds for providing barracks, we conclude that the expense of the alterations in the above house will be defrayed out of the private purses of the Magistrates.

On the 14th of October *The Cambrian* reported that,

notwithstanding the Royal proclamation and the removal of obnoxious gates and bars, outrages still proceed in the Principality ... On Monday last [9th of October] the detachment of the 76th Regiment, stationed in this town under the command of Major Halifax, embarked on board the 'Dee', government steamer, which had arrived at Swansea on Friday last, having left Plymouth on the previous day ... On her voyage to Swansea, she was run into by a schooner, and one of her paddle-boxes damaged ... A light company of the 73rd, who are to be stationed at Pontardulais and Pontyberem [in Carmarthenshire] left Swansea for those places yesterday morning. – A few days ago, about fifty of the London police left the City for Wales.

Thomas Penrice's Letters

A retired major, Thomas Penrice of Kilvrough was a big landowner in the Gower Peninsula. He was gentry, a magistrate, a Swansea Turnpike trustee and a persistent letter writer. More than a few of his letters were published by *The Cambrian* – all of them in connection with toll-gates and related subjects. It is plain from these letters that Thomas was at odds with his fellow magistrates, his fellow trustees and the Secretary of State; moreover, he thoroughly disapproved of Captain Napier and the Rural Police. The only people he seems to have been in tune with were ordinary people, particularly when he saw them as oppressed.

In September he wrote numerous letters, the first in support of the Penclawdd cockle-women, arguing against tolls on donkeys. On the 14th of October, *The Cambrian* published no less than seven of his letters, all of them in connection with what he saw as an unjust imposition on the ratepayers of the parishes of Pennard and Ilston. Shortly after the attack on the Poundffald gate, Captain Napier had assigned twelve locally appointed parish constables to guard the Kilvrough and Cartersford toll-gates for a period of five weeks.

After the twelve constables had been discharged of their duties, the ratepayers in the two parishes – within which the gates were sited – were saddled with the expense of paying the constables wages. Thomas considered the imposition as unjust and, as

> the proprietor of the greatest part of both these parishes ... endeavoured to protect the interests of [his] tenants ... The Kilvrough Gate [which was] put up a few years ago [was] not likely to be destroyed by the parishioners themselves ... [as they were descended from] a colony of Flemings that settled here in the time of Henry the Second. [Thomas admitted that there had] been some foolish alerts ... caused by some boys firing off fowling pieces ... to annoy the Rural police-force ... [but] it would be more just if the Turnpike Trustees were made to pay for the protection of their property.

Thomas's letters did not resolve the situation, as the demand for payment was to continue for many weeks to come.

The Queen's Proclamation

By October there was a noticeable reduction in the number of attacks carried out by Rebecca. There were several reasons for this. At the end of July it had become known that the government was prepared to listen to the grievances. In August growing numbers gave their support to mass meetings and other non-violent means of making their point. In September many farmers became alarmed by the escalating violence. Then, on the 2nd of October, the Queen put her signature to a proclamation.

The essence of this proclamation were rewards. A reward of £500 was available to 'any person who shall discover and apprehend the ... perpetrators ... of any ... outrages' connected with Rebecca. The purpose of this huge reward was to encourage law-enforcement officers to maximise their efforts, and Captain Napier fell into this category. He had been ridiculed by the London press for his fight with 'the old woman with a frying pan', and at least one newspaper was to portray him as a villain for gunning down 'poor farmers' sons' and their horses. Parliament, however, not only presented Napier with £500, but it passed a vote of thanks for his services. One wonders whether the government could not have made better use of such a sum.

A smaller reward, coupled with a pardon, was aimed at encouraging law-breakers – except those who were the actual perpetrators of an outrage – to inform on each other. The reward was £50 'for each and every person who shall be so convicted [of an offence] and shall receive our most gracious pardon for the said offence'. This lesser reward led to a spate of arrests, the result of unscrupulous men informing on others before someone informed on them.

On the 25th of October a three-man Royal Commission arrived at Carmarthen, from whence it began a tour of South Wales. The purpose of this commission was to establish the cause of the discontent and – more importantly – to make recommendation on how to remedy the situation. The Commission took five months to complete its work. In the meantime another Royal Commission would concentrate on doing the dirty work.

CHAPTER FIVE

Trials by Special Commission

There was an Assize Court at the Townhall, Swansea, but due to the fact that a jury made up of local people was likely to be either intimidated, or sympathetic towards the 17 persons awaiting trial, it was decided to hold the trials at Cardiff, where jurors were less likely – so it was thought – to be biased or influenced by intimidation; moreover, owing to the seriousness of the situation it was decided that the trials would be by a special commission, rather than wait for the customary Spring Assizes.

On Thursday the 26th of October 'the Special Commission was opened ... in the Townhall [Cardiff]'. For security reasons 'a strong detachment of the A division of London Police' were present when, with great pomp and ceremony, the government-appointed Judges, the 75-year-old Mr. Baron Gurney, and the younger and more charitable Sir Cresswell Cresswell, arrived 'at eleven o'clock in the High Sheriff's carriage, escorted by several of the neighbouring gentry in their carriages. Their Lordships immediately proceeded to the Townhall to open the Commission ... the court was then ... adjourned to two o'clock'.

There were 17 people due to appear before the Judges, but it was said that some of them – those who faced the lesser charge of destroying certain turnpike gates – would not be tried. However, all were there, 'ready to surrender, if called upon'. The defendants were to be represented by a 'very eminent Counsel' – M. D. Hill, Q. C., a radical law reformer, and three other barristers.

'Soon after two o'clock, the Learned Judges took their seats on the bench ... The Common Jury list was then called over'. This jury – which had proved difficult to form in the face of numerous refusals – was eventually made up of gentlemen and tradesmen from Cardiff and Merthyr; farmers were excluded.

On Friday the 2nd of November, the prisoner, 'John Hughes was ... placed at the bar ... his arm in a sling'. The charges were read over: that, one, he did unlawfully, riotously and tumultuously assemble with divers others, to the disturbance of the peace; that, two, he did feloniously, unlawfully and with force begin to demolish and pull down the dwelling house of one William Lewis (the toll-collector); and, three, that he did shoot at one C. F. Napier with intent feloniously and with malice afterthought to kill and murder him. To all three charges John Hughes pleaded, 'Not Guilty'.

Apart from a few technicalities, there was no real defence against the overwhelming evidence that was brought against him – both verbal and in the form of implements picked up after the affray. Some of the verbal evidence was not reported by *The Cambrian* when Hughes stood before magistrates at Swansea. This additional evidence gives further insight into what actually happened at Pontardulais.

Captain Napier said that, with regard to Rebecca's intentions,

> I had received the information about four o'clock that evening ... We went across the country, starting at Penllergaer, about ten o'clock ... [We] had to walk ten or eleven miles ... on foot ... [during which time] I heard a great noises of horns blown ... and firing ... We halted in the field about 600 yards from the gate. While in the field, I heard first of all a great noise of voices ... on the Carmarthen side [of the river]. The noise increased considerably and came from the direction of the Red Lion Inn ... [eventually] some of the mob cried out, 'Gate, gate'. It was now ten minutes to one o'clock ... I heard sounds of gate-breaking and the smashing of glass. I then ordered my men to follow me, and proceeded across the lane, and then to the main road.

Left: *Despite his 'soft' features, Captain Charles Frederick Napier was a very capable Chief Constable and a man of action. He was born in Ceylon in 1805. At the age of 21 he joined the Rifle Brigade. In 1841 he applied for the post of Glamorgan's first Chief Constable; as such he recruited, trained and equipped a force of four superintendents and 34 constables. The force not only grew in number, but it was regarded as the most efficient in Wales. Aged 62, he died from T.B. in January 1867, after catching a cold whilst waiting for a train at Cardiff.*

When counsel for the defence addressed the Jury the following day, he referred back to Captain Napier's evidence, saying

> that information of the intended attack ... had been given as early as four o'clock that evening, and that after a delay [for] which no explanation had been given, the police had proceeded armed ... with pistols [cutlasses] ... knowing ... that a crime was contemplated, [and] instead of making any attempt to prevent the riot, they were ... hiding in the field until the gate had been broken ... Here the magistrates and police had an opportunity of preventing a great outrage of the law, but instead of doing so, they waited to see it committed.

The implication was obvious – Captain Napier wanted to make arrests, not prevent a crime. This premise was supported by the prosecutors' statement that 'it was Captain Napier's object to wound the horses, so as to apprehend the riders'. As for when Captain Napier moved down the road on the Swansea side of the gate; he said:

> I saw three men mounted, disguised, with their horses facing the toll-house ... The men of horseback appeared to be directing the other parties [on the other side of the gate] ... I ordered my men to fall in, and advanced towards the party, and cried out, 'Stop, stop, stop', as loud as I could. One of the men on horseback appeared to hear, fired at me. I then said, 'Mark that man'. I advanced with my pistol and fired at the horse ... The horses turned, and the party appeared as if they rode [at] us. The man on the horse I shot fell ... I then advanced to him and we struggled. He was then wounded in the arm, but by whom I know not ... I did not take that person into custody ... as I was struck with a stick on the back of the head. The person I was struggling with had a straw hat and a loose white dress, similar to a Druid's dress ... I afterwards saw the same man in the custody of one of the police.

What happened to John Hughes after that appears in the later evidence given by P. C. John Price, who deposed: 'I then apprehended John Hughes, who said, "Let me go, you have broken my arm already".'

Parts of the evidence given by J. D. Llewelyn, one of the magistrates, are of interest 'Afterwards, I saw the man who had been taken with two others into custody – the prisoner [John Hughes] is one ... I went to the inn to procure water for the prisoners, and bandages, and conveyances to take them to Swansea'.

On the following day more witnesses were called, after which, counsel for the defence gave a 'most appropriate, eloquent and feeling address [to the jury]. Eleven witnesses were then called, who gave the prisoner a character for general good conduct and obedience to the laws'. It was all to no avail. When the jury returned after 15 to 20 minutes deliberation, their verdict was 'GUILTY – with a strong recommendation to mercy on account of previous good character. Sentence [was] deferred' until Monday when it would be revealed that 'mercy' was a word that Judge Gurney did not understand.

Harsh Sentencing

On Monday the 30th of October:

> David Jones and John Hugh were placed at the bar ... The officer of the Court ... read over the indictment, charging them with having unlawfully, riotously and tumultuously assembled together, to the disturbance of the peace, and feloniously, unlawfully and with force began to demolish and pull down the dwelling house of one William Lewis. [In response], both prisoners ... in a hesitating manner, pleaded, 'Not Guilty', but after a short conversation between the Counsel on both sides ... the Clerk ... repeated the question, to which the prisoners, having retracted their original plea, pleaded 'Guilty'.
> The Attorney General then rose ... [and] begged to enter a 'nolle prosequi' as far as all other charges against the prisoners were' concerned, presumably because he knew Judge Gurney would be merciless.

The defence counsellor, Mr. Hill, Q.C., 'then proceeded to address the Court in mitigation of punishment ...'

> With respect to ... John Hughes, he begged to call ... attention to the excellent character he had received; and he could confidently state, that the same observations were equally applicable to the other two ... [moreover] John Hughes had been wounded in the arm ... [and] that had produced a permanent disability ... With regard to ... David Jones, there were at the present time in his body several slugs, which the medical men were unable to extract.

Mr. Hill spoke of a spirit of mercy, of reconciliation and much more, but to no avail. Judge Gurney was of the opinion that:

> an example must be made ... for the purpose of deterring others from the commission of such crimes ... it is [therefore] impossible to inflict a less sentence upon you, David Jones and John Hugh, than 'transportation for seven years.' [And] with regard to you, John Hughes ... the sentence cannot be lighter than 'transportation for twenty years.'

The trial then continued and:

Margaret Morgan, aged 25, Morgan Morgan, 57, Esther Morgan, 63, Rees Morgan, 23, and John Morgan, 21, were then placed at the bar, on a charge of having assaulted Capt. C. F. Napier, in the execution of his duty, and in having endeavoured to prevent the lawful apprehension of one Henry Morgan. On the usual questions being put, all the prisoners pleaded, 'Guilty'. They were also charged with common assault.

The Attorney General [said] he would not pray for sentence on Morgan and Esther Morgan, but in the three other cases he thought, though not a severe one, some sentence commensurate with the offence was necessary. The father and mother – [in view of] their advanced age – having entered into their own recognizance to appear and receive judgement [at a later date] ... were discharged.

Mr. Hill begged to remind the Court that one of the prisoners [John] had suffered severely from a gun-shot wound, [but] his Lordship ... observed ... it is most important that officers should be protected in the execution of their duty ... [he] then sentenced Margaret Morgan to six months imprisonment, Rees Morgan and John Morgan to twelve months each, and added, 'The Court having received information that ... your character has been good, is the only reason that hard labour is not added to your sentence'.

Lewis Davies pleaded guilty to the charge of having, with others, riotously assembled and assisted in the destruction of Pontardulais gate. The Attorney General said ... he would not pray for judgement on the defendant, providing he would enter into his own recognizance to appear [at a later date] ... the defendant was discharged.

The Attorney General also said, that in looking over the deposition relating to the charges against David Lewis for having assaulted the toll-collector on the Tycoch Gate, he begged to enter a 'nolle prosequi'. [The reason for this is not stated, but it is likely that Margaret Arnold (the toll-collector) failed to appear as a witness.]

The non-appearance of another witness may have been the reason why the trial of six other Gowerians did not take place, being deferred until the Spring Assizes. The six men were alleged to have been involved in the destruction of the Bolgoed and Rhyd-y-pandy gates. The only witnesses to their involvement was the informer, John Jones, and if he failed to appear, then the prosecution would have been unable to proceed.

The boy, William Hughes, [who was arrested in connection with the Pontardulais gate] was then discharged by proclamation, no true bill having been found against him.

Saddled with Unfair Expenses

On the 2nd of December *The Cambrian* reported that magistrates were presented with:

> a petition which was numerously and repeatedly signed by the parishioners of Pennard, Gower, protesting against an order signed by J.D. Llewelyn ... and several other Magistrates, by which the parishioners were saddled with the expenses incurred by watching the [Kilvrough / Vennaway] gate by the constables during the late outrages on the part of 'Rebecca and her daughters', and expressing a hope that the same would be countermanded.
>
> Mr. Attwood [Clerk to the Magistrates] stated, that some time ago ... he was requested to write [about this matter] to the Secretary of State ... [whose answer was] to the effect that the parishioners were liable ... Since then, said Mr. Attwood, there had been a correspondence upon the same subject, between Mr. Penrice of Kilvrough and the Secretary of State, and the latter went so far as to state that he [Mr. Penrice] had no right to interfere. [The parishioners' representative] thought it to be a very hard case that the parishioners should pay, particularly as there was no 'Rebecca' in the neighbourhood. [One magistrate reminded the representative] that a gate in the neighbourhood [the Poundffald] had been destroyed, and that many respectable farmers had declined paying tolls in passing through the Pennard gate.

A Pennard parishioner who was present remarked, 'We be quiet people – we had no riots since the world began'. After some further conversation ... the application was dismissed.

Transportation

Just before Christmas *The Cambrian* reported:

> John Hugh, John Hughes and David Jones, convicted at the last Special Commission at Cardiff for the destruction of Pontardulais bridge toll-house, were sent off on Wednesday [7th December] ... from the county gaol, pursuant to their sentences ... with a view of being forwarded to their destination.

This is *The Cambrian's* last reference to the three prisoners involved in the Pontardulais shootout. As to the fate of those unfortunate men the reader will find well-researched and detailed accounts of their suffering in far more extensive work than this one. Two of the best are: *The Rebecca Riots* by David Williams, *And They Blessed Rebecca* by Pat Malloy.

Briefly, the prisoners were taken to the notorious Millbank Penitentiary in London, where they endured three months of strict discipline and a maddening solitude in which even the guards were not permitted to speak to them. Petitions were sent to the Queen, begging for a reduction in John Hughes's sentence; they were sent by his mother and even members of the jury who had found him guilty – to no avail. All three men were put aboard the convict ship *London* and, on the 12th of March 1844, they set sail to endure a horrendous four-month voyage to Van Dieman's Land (Tasmania). They arrived at their destination on the 10th of July 1844. A week later David Jones, the young man who still had several slugs in his back, was dead.

John Hugh served his seven-year sentence as a slave, being freed in December 1850. Two years later he married a convict woman – presumably his Carmarthenshire wife had died by then. John Hughes served only 13½ years of his 20-year sentence, receiving a conditional pardon in 1857. He often wrote home, but never made the return journey. He married and made a life for himself in Tasmania, dying at the turn of the century at the ripe old age of 82.

The Glamorgan Spring Assizes

Meanwhile, back home, the remaining seven Gowerians appeared at the Glamorgan Spring Assizes. In March 1844, 'no bills were preferred [meaning the charges were dropped] against Griffith Vaughan, William Morgan, David Jones [and] Daniel Lewis' for their alleged involvement in the destruction of the Bolgoed gate, and 'no bills were preferred against Matthew Morgan [and] Henry Morgan' for their alleged involvement in the destruction of the Rhyd-y-pandy gate. Why no bills were preferred against these six men is not stated, but it is likely that either the informer, John Jones, was discredited as a witness, or that he failed to turn up at court. Either way the prosecution was left without its one and only witness.

David Lewis, the collier alleged to have been involved in the destruction of the Tycoch gate, St. Thomas, was not mentioned. It has been said that he was discharged by royal proclamation on the 13th of March 1844, although no evidence of this can be found in *The Cambrian*. If he was discharged – due to the non-appearance of the witness Margaret Arnold – then he really was the luckiest of men, for he had assaulted Margaret, the toll-collector, and for that he could have been sentenced to transportation.

In July 1844 the Swansea magistrates were authorized to present John Jones with a gratuity of £20 under the terms of the Queen's proclamation. Almost two years later (14th of April 1846) *The Cambrian* reported that 'John Jones, the informer ... whose apprehension by our police on a charge of stealing a brass pan at Pontardulais ... was tried at Carmarthen Quarter Sessions ... and acquitted by the jury, the evidence being defective. Jones [had] admitted his guilt to Sergeant Bennet of the Swansea police force, who apprehended him on suspicion, having detected him while offering the article for sale to a marine store-dealer in this town. Through some oversight Mr. Bennet was not subpoenaed as a witness'. After that, John Jones vanishes from the records.

The Report of the Commission of Inquiry

On the 6th of March 1844 the long-awaited *Report of the Commission of Inquiry* appeared in print. The report stated that 'we [the commissioners] assembled at Carmarthen on the 25th day of October last ... [and] terminated our inquiries at Merthyr Tydvil on the 13th day of December'. Only fragments of the report are given here; they are as follows:-

The commissioners were able to declare with:

> great satisfaction ... that the disturbances ... were not connected with political causes ... [but were] first stimulated by a sense of local grievances ... and the spirit, once roused, was perverted in some instances by evil-disposed persons ... The chief grounds of complaint were the mismanagement of the funds applicable to turnpike roads, the frequency and the amount of the payment of tolls and, in some cases, the vexatious conduct of toll-collectors and the illegal demands made by them. [Tithes, rent, Poor Law and] the administration of justice by the local magistrates [were added grievances at a time when] a succession of wet and unproductive harvests had very much reduced the capital of the farmers ... [and also] the price of sheep, cattle and butter had fallen.

With regard to Glamorganshire, there were several independent trusts, although all of them conformed to

> one uniform rate of toll ... with reference to the Swansea district [it was noted] that between that town and Llanelly, four tolls are paid on eleven miles of road, two to the Swansea Trust, one at Loughor Bridge, and one to the Kidwelly Trust ... Between Swansea and Neath, a distance of nine miles, three gates are payable. This ... arises from the circumstances of the Wych Tree Trust being established by a separate Act of Parliament ... [and this act] has thwarted all attempts which have been made to consolidate the [two] trusts ... [and remove] the Wych Tree Gate.

The commissioners concluded:

> that in order to remove the existing discontent, and to remedy the ... present system, some important changes must be made in laws

relating to roads ... [It is, however, right] that those who use the roads should contribute to their upkeep ... [We, therefore, propose] that in the counties of Carmarthen, Pembroke and Glamorgan ... the establishment of consolidated trusts for each county ... [that] a moderate and uniform rate of toll should be established in the consolidated trusts ... [that] the most convenient position of the turnpike-gates [be] determined on, and the ... frequency of the demands for payment got rid of ... Should, however, the money levied at the turnpike-gates prove insufficient to provide for all ... [expenses], then the deficiency ... should be made good by a rate upon all property now liable to poor and highway rate ... [It is also] desirable to repeal, with respect to South Wales, all the laws ... which now exist for the regulation of turnpike-roads ... [as well as] placing all the trusts in each county under one general executive [later to become known as the Roads Board].

As a general rule, toll should not be paid oftener than once in seven or eight miles in the same county ... [but] on the confines of two counties ... the gates in different trusts ... should reciprocally clear each other within a definite, but shorter distance. [With regard to bridges] on the confines of two counties [as at Loughor] the expense of maintaining such structures should be apportioned between the two [county trusts. So] the gate now standing on the bridge should be continued.

Due to innumerable difficulties, the new Glamorgan Roads Boards did not come into existence until 1845, by which time many of the toll-gates within the Lordship of Gower and Kilvey had ceased to function. Other gates remained in place for 30 years, primarily to pay off the debts of the old turnpike trusts. Then, in 1876, the remaining gates were all discontinued and the roads taken over by the Glamorgan Highways Board.

Rebecca, then, had achieved her aim – the removal of unnecessary gates, a reduction in the rate of toll, and the curbing of the arbitrary powers of the turnpike trustees. Above all the Lady had forced the government to listen and to remedy the situation. True, there had been a price to pay by a small number her of daughters who had received harsh sentences, and there was also a small 'evil-disposed' element who had tarnished the Lady's image; moreover, the ratepayers were saddled with expenses for many years to come – expenses to do with the billeting of troops, as well as the wages of London policemen and local militia – but by and large Rebecca was truly a people's protest, one that has become firmly established as an important part of Welsh history. She has certainly left an indelible mark on the people who live in localities where those extraordinary events took place.

BY THE SAME AUTHOR

A History of Gower
ISBN 1 873827 13 X
162 pp. Illustrated. Card cover
Logaston Press, 2002
Out of print, but still to be found in local libraries

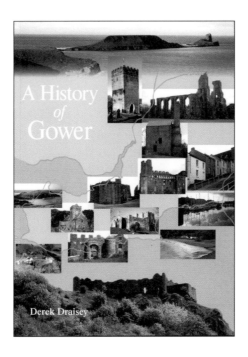

This book covers the history of Gower and Swansea from Roman times to the mid-19th century. It tells of Celtic saints, of how the Welsh lived before and after the arrival of Anglo-Norman conquistadors. With the aid of maps and pictures, it gives insight into how the landscape was shaped by English settlement and how Swansea came into existence. For 200 years the battle lines were drawn, castles attacked, towns burned, to be followed by plagues and finally a more peaceful coexistence, both side benefiting from the growing prosperity of Tudor times.

Swansea had a part to play during the Civil War, gun-running for the King and changing sides in the face of opposing forces. In the 18th century smugglers were active in the peninsula, and the growing coal industry in the Swansea Valley was to lay the foundations of Swansea's expansion to become the copper metropolis of the world, home of the Vivians and other industrial magnates.

BY THE SAME AUTHOR

The People of Gower
ISBN 0 9546544 0 4
136 pp. Illustrated. Card cover
Draisey Publishing 2003. £5.00

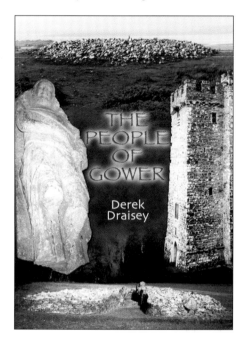

This book tells the story of man's presence in the Gower Peninsula and its upland extension between the Tawe and Loughor rivers. What happened in this unique area, where man's past achievements in earth and stone abound, is a reflection, albeit on a smaller scale, of the rise and fall of successive cultures that existed in Wales and, indeed, mainland Britain from Stone Age times to c.1400.

The people who spearheaded these intrusive, often invasive cultures settled, initially, in relatively small numbers in the coastal lowlands where they coexisted with, and eventually imposed much of their cultural identities on the indigenous inhabitants, leaving the natives in the upland areas to carry on in their time-honoured ways for centuries until they, too, became absorbed into the intrusive cultures.

BY THE SAME AUTHOR

Women in Welsh History

ISBN 0 9546544 1 2
205 pp. Illustrated. Card cover
Draisey Publishing 2004. £6.50

Most of what has been recorded of the past reflects the perceptions of men. Consequently, women have been marginalized. This book is, therefore, an attempt to give the women of Wales a rightful place in their country's history, from Celtic times to the present day.

The names and achievements of many outstanding women are to be found within these pages – and more: this is the story of women throughout the ages, both rich and poor, of courtship, marriage, childbearing, abortion, crime, employment, dress and a host of other issues that were, and continue to be, relevant to the women of Wales.

BY THE SAME AUTHOR

The Last Lord of Gower
A Prophecy Unfolds
ISBN 0 9546544 2 0
203 pp. Maps & plans. Card cover
Draisey Publishing 2005. £5.00

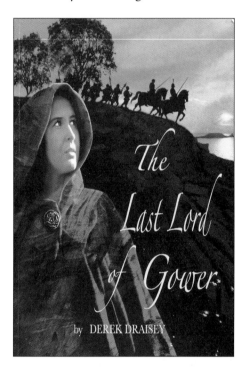

Set in 12th century Gower, the heart of this sinewy tale is based on the camaraderie shared by two foster brothers in their struggle to remain free from foreign rule. Running parallel to scenes of bloody conflict is an eternal triangle; when the foster brothers were youths it was Maredudd who first won Gwenllian's affection; at her father's insistence she married Rhydderch with whom she finds a different, more mature relationship – but the embers of her love for Maredudd still smoulder.

The invasion of Gower is led by two Norman-French knights; the resolute William de Londres and the brutal theomaniac, Henry de Viles, each seeking to outdo the other in terrorizing the native population into submission – but they have, first, to contend with Rhydderch's uncle, Rhys, Lord of Gower, and while he takes steps to offer battle, the foster brothers confound the invaders in several well-placed ambushes.

BY THE SAME AUTHOR

Gower Rogues
ISBN 0 9546544 3 9
248 pp. Illustrated. Card cover
Draisey Publishing 2006. £6.50

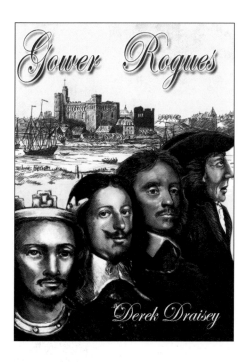

From the 12th century onwards the Lordship of Gower was more often the property of Anglo-Norman and English lords. At times it was held by kings of England, occasionally by Welsh princes, and for eleven years by Oliver Cromwell. Many of these men were rogues. The infamous King John requires no introduction, but his crony William de Breos, who succeeded him as Lord of Gower, became notorious for his greed and his murderous attacks on Welshmen. A later Welsh lord, Rhys Grug, engaged in ethnic cleansing.

Few of these lords resided at Swansea Castle, which for centuries served as the administrative centre of the lordship. The administrative and judicial affairs of Gower were in the hands of stewards, many of whom abused their positions to enrich themselves or enforce their will. One of the worst offenders was Sir George Herbert, who had no qualms about judicial murder. A more questionable rogue was Colonel Philip Jones who made hay while the sun shone, and who became one of the most powerful men in the realm. Gabriel Powell, on the other hand, was one steward who simply wanted all his own way.

BY THE SAME AUTHOR

The Last Lord of Gower
Part Two, A Thorn in Flesh
ISBN 0 9546544 4 3
290 pp. Maps & plans. Card cover
Draisey Publishing 2007. £6.50

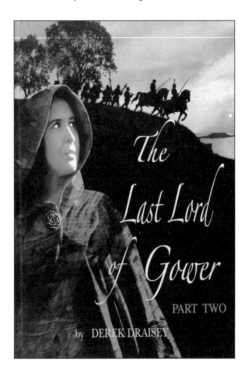

Ten years of relative peace have passed since Henry de Beaumont's invasion of Gower; now it is 1116, another year with a cursed six as its last number. For Rhydderch the trouble starts when a disinherited prince marches on Gower to attack the castle at Abertawe, thereby presenting him with the dilemma of whether or not to rebel. Rhydderch is not involved in the attack himself, but members of his household are, reason for his arch-enemies – the madman Henry de Viles and the resolute William de Londres – to insist that action be taken against him. His position is exacerbated by the soothsayer's prophecy that someone close to him will die, and by the fact that someone is informing on his covert activities to forge unity among fellow Countrymen far and wide.